There's a Rainbow in the River

By Phil Cummings

Illustrated by Margaret Power

BEN RAN AS FAST AS HE COULD.
His black boots swished through the wet
grass. Annie and Tom were close behind.

It was Saturday morning and they were on
their way to the park.

When they reached the gate, Ben shouted,
"First one to the river!" and the race began.

The river was their favorite place. It was really only a gentle stream but they liked to call it a river.

They spent a lot of time by the river, watching the water jump, splash, and twist its way through the park. They liked the noises it made and the way the river sparkled in the sunlight. Tom said it looked like silver paper and, sometimes, it did.

Down the grassy bank and under the huge trees they ran.

"I'll beat you all!" Ben cried. "And I'll find the first frog."

"No, you won't. I will," said Annie, her long hair flapping as she ran.

"It's not fair!" yelled Tom, Annie's little brother. "I can't keep up."

They were on their way to catch frogs and tadpoles. They had caught them many times before in the river and knew just where to look. They looked in pools hidden away in reeds and rocks, and found muddy places where the frogs liked to play.

Annie was the best frog-catcher. Ben was good at catching tadpoles while Tom got very messy helping them both. Whenever they caught something, they'd watch it for a while in a jar or bucket then let it go.

Sometimes, they took tadpoles home and watched them change into frogs before bringing them back to the river. Ben had a wonderful old aquarium that he kept them in.

Ben was the first one to run under the bridge that crossed the river. This was the best spot.

The water was almost still as it trickled over a wall of rocks. There were a lot of reeds and the water was shaded by the bridge and a huge old tree.

When Ben knelt by the river with his bucket and net, he saw something swirling on top of the water.

He moved his head from side to side and saw rainbows.

"Hey, come here!" he called to Annie and Tom. "There's a rainbow in the river."

Annie and Tom looked into the river and saw the faint rainbows shimmering on top of the water.

"What is it?" asked Tom.

"I don't know," said Ben. "But it's beautiful, isn't it?"

"It is," said Annie, putting her hand in the water to scoop up a rainbow.

But, when Annie took her hand out, it wasn't covered with rainbows. It was speckled with slimy black oil.

"Oh, yuck!" said Tom. "What's that?"

Ben scooped some onto his hand and looked at it closely. "It's oil," he said, wiping his hand on his jeans.

Annie was worried about the frogs and tadpoles. She gently stirred the water with a stick.

"This oil will kill the frogs and tadpoles if we don't do something about it," she cried. "We've got to find out where it's coming from!"

"You're right!" said Ben, quickly. "I hope we're not too late."

"Come on then," said Tom. "Let's go!"

So they began walking quickly upstream, staying close to the bank.

They climbed over rocks and clung to the roots of trees, hundreds of years old. In some places, the bank was slippery and they nearly fell in.

They hadn't gone far when Ben found some dirty water trickling down a steep bank and into the river.

"Here it is!" he cried, pointing to the top of the bank. "It's coming from up there."

"Let's climb up and see if we can stop it," said Annie.

"Wait for me," said Tom.

The three friends climbed the bank as quickly as they could. When they reached the top, they found themselves at the end of their own street. They saw the water coming through a pipe under the road.

"Look!" Tom said, suddenly. "Look over there!"

Annie and Ben looked to where Tom was pointing.

They saw Mr. Buckley, one of their neighbors, spraying his driveway with a hose. Mr. Buckley had been fixing his car and his driveway was black with oil.

The oil from Mr. Buckley's driveway was gurgling into the drain, flowing under the road, and finding its way into the river.

Ben, Annie, and Tom all cried out together, "STOP! MR. BUCKLEY, STOP!"

Mr. Buckley looked up in surprise when he heard them. "What is it?" he asked. "What's wrong?"

The three friends ran to tell him.

"You're killing the tadpoles," Tom said, puffing.

"I'm what?" said Mr. Buckley, frowning.

They quickly told Mr. Buckley how his oil was finding its way into the river.

Mr. Buckley felt awful. He had caught frogs and tadpoles in the river when he was a boy. It was still one of his favorite places.

"Oh dear," he said, turning off the hose. "I didn't know. I just wanted to clean my driveway."

"We've got to get back to the river and save as many frogs and tadpoles as we can," said Annie.

Mr. Buckley ran into his house. "I'll call for help, then I'll come, too," he said.

Mr. Buckley wasn't very good at catching tadpoles or frogs. He kept falling over, like Tom.

He was a mess by the time help arrived to begin the cleanup.

Annie, Ben, Tom, and Mr. Buckley went to Mr. Buckley's place to check on the tadpoles and frogs they had saved. Mr. Buckley put them in his bathtub, sink, and anywhere he could find.

So the next time Annie, Ben, and Tom went to the river, Mr. Buckley went with them, and so did a crowd of other people who lived on the street.

They all had their buckets, tubs, and jars full of tadpoles and frogs they had collected from Mr. Buckley's house.

And they let them go in a clean river that sparkled in the sunshine like silver paper.